MY CAT

Me and My
PET

By William Anthony

BookLife
PUBLISHING

©2019
BookLife Publishing Ltd.
King's Lynn
Norfolk PE30 4LS

A catalogue record for this book is available from the British Library.

ISBN: 978-1-78637-571-1

Written by:
William Anthony

Edited by:
Robin Twiddy

Designed by:
Jasmine Pointer

CONTENTS

Words that look like **this** can be found in the glossary on page 24.

Amy ♥ and Lola

Amy

Lola

Hello! My name's Amy, and this is my pet cat, Lola. She's five years old. Cats are my favourite animal because they're soft and furry, and they are fun to play with!

Whether you're thinking about getting a cat, or you've had one for a little while, Lola and I are going to take you through how to look after them!

Getting a Cat

Looking after a pet cat means you are going to have a lot of **responsibility**. You will need to feed them, and give them a nice home with a comfy bed and lots of toys!

My family got Lola from a rescue centre, but you can get cats from lots of places. You can get a cat from a breeder. This is someone who keeps cats to **mate** them.

Rescue centres help cats find new families.

Home

Cats need lots of space to explore at home! Cats also like to explore outside, so make sure you let them outside if you don't have a cat flap!

Cats can be very **independent**.

Cats have a very good sense of direction. They can almost always find their way back home, so you shouldn't worry about your cat getting lost outside.

It's almost like a secret super power!

Playtime

Lola likes to play with feathers!

Lola loves to play, just like all cats do! Sometimes they like to play with toys on their own and other times they like to play with humans too.

Cats like to try and catch things. You could make a scrunchy ball from paper to use during playtime, or get them to try and catch a ball of string!

Make sure you play gently with your cat so you don't hurt them!

Food

All of that fun will make your cat very hungry, so you need to leave a bowl of food out on the floor for them.

Cat treats help cats know when they've done something good.

Cats need to eat meat to be healthy. You can buy dry pet food or tinned meat at the pet shop. There are different foods for different ages – kitten, adult and **senior**.

Bedtime $^{zZ^Z}$

zzzZZ!

Cats get sleepy just like we do. Most cats can sleep for up to 16 hours every day! Every time I see Lola she seems to be taking a nap!

Because cats sleep a lot, it's important to give them a nice bed to sleep in. You could buy a comfy cat bed from a pet shop or set out some soft, fluffy blankets.

Did you know cats snore just like humans?

The Vet

Vets are like doctors, but for animals instead of humans!

Cats can get ill, just like humans. Cats that are ill can go to the vets. The vet will do everything they can to help your cat get better again!

If you think your cat isn't very well,
make sure you tell someone.

One day when I came home, Lola was very tired and didn't want to eat. I told my parents and we took her to the vet, who made her all better again!

Growing Up

When a cat gets old, they will not want to play as much. Older cats will want to sleep more because they will get tired more easily.

Cats get weaker when they are old, so they need even more care.

It's very important to take even more care of cats when they're old. You need to be very gentle with them, and always make sure they're comfortable.

Super Cats

Some cats are simply super. A cat called Merlin has a purr that's nearly 70 decibels (say: deh-sih-bells). That's as loud as a vacuum cleaner!

PURRRRR!

Look
out
below!

A cat in the US landed the biggest jump by a cat ever, which was over 60 metres. That's like a human jumping down from the top of eight houses all stacked on top of each other!

You ♥ and Your Pet

Whether your cat is a normal cat or a super cat, make sure you take care of them just like Lola and I have taught you!

I'm sure you'll make a great pet owner. Try to come up with some fun games to play with your cat, and most of all, have fun with your new fluff ball!

GLOSSARY

decibels	units for measuring sound
independent	able to look after yourself
mate	to produce young with an animal of the same species
responsibility	having tasks that you are expected to do
senior	an old person or animal

INDEX

24